THE COMPLETE POEMS
OF ANNE BRONTE

Edited by CLEMENT SHORTER

A Digireads.com Book
Digireads.com Publishing

The Complete Poems of Anne Bronte
By Anne Bronte
Edited by Clement Shorter
ISBN 10: 1-4209-4396-0
ISBN 13: 978-1-4209-4396-2

Please visit *www.digireads.com*

INTRODUCTION[1]

BY CHARLOTTE BRONTË

In looking over my sister Anne's papers, I find mournful evidence that religious feeling had been to her but too much like what it was to Cowper; I mean, of course, in a far milder form. Without rendering her a prey to those horrors that defy concealment, it subdued her mood and bearing to a perpetual pensiveness; the pillar of a cloud glided constantly before her eyes; she ever waited at the foot of a secret Sinai, listening in her heart to the voice of a trumpet sounding long and waxing louder. Some, perhaps, would rejoice over these tokens of sincere though sorrowing piety in a deceased relative: I own, to me they seem sad, as if her whole innocent life had been passed under the martyrdom of an unconfessed physical pain: their effect, indeed, would be too distressing, were it not combated by the certain knowledge that in her last moments this tyranny of a too tender conscience was overcome; this pomp of terrors broke up, and passing away, left her dying hour unclouded. Her belief in God did not then bring to her dread, as of a stern Judge,—but hope, as in a Creator and Saviour: and no faltering hope was it, but a sure and stedfast conviction, on which, in the rude passage from Time to Eternity, she threw the weight of her human weakness, and by which she was enabled to bear what was to be borne, patiently—serenely—victoriously.

---

[1] Prefixed to *Selections from Poems by Acton Bell,* first published in the 1850 edition of *Wuthering Heights* and *Agnes Grey.*

CONTENTS

6

THE CAPTAIN'S DREAM

Methought I saw him but I knew him not;
He was so changed from what he used to be,
There was no redness on his woe-worn cheek,
No sunny smile upon his ashy lips,
His hollow wandering eyes looked wild and fierce,
And grief was printed on his marble brow,
And, oh, I thought he claspéd his wasted hands,
And raised his haggard eyes to Heaven, and prayed
That he might die—I had no power to speak,
I thought I was allowed to see him thus;
And yet I might not speak one single word;
I might not even tell him that I lived
And that it might be possible if search were made,
To find out where I was and set me free,
Oh! how I longed to clasp him to my heart,
Or but to hold his trembling hand in mine,
And speak one word of comfort to his mind,
I struggled wildly but it was in vain,
I could not rise from my dark dungeon floor,
And the dear name I vainly strove to speak,
Died in a voiceless whisper on my tongue.
Then I awoke, and lo! it was a dream!
A dream? Alas it was reality!
For well I know wherever he may be
He mourns me thus—O heaven I could bear
My deadly fate with calmness if there were
No kindred hearts to bleed and break for me!

THE NORTH WIND

That wind is from the North, I know it well;
No other breeze could have so wild a swell.
Now deep and loud it thunders round my cell,
    The faintly dies, and softly sighs,
And moans and murmurs mournfully.
I know its language; thus is speaks to me—

'I have passed over thy own mountains dear,
    Thy northern mountains—and they still are free,
Still lonely, wild, majestic, bleak and drear,
    And stern and lovely, as they used to be

When thou, a young enthusiast,
  As wild and free as they,
O'er rocks and glens and snowy heights
  Didst often love to stray.

I've blown the wild untrodden snows
  In whirling eddies from their brows,
And I have howled in caverns wild
Where thou, a joyous mountain child,
  Didst dearly love to be.
The sweet world is not changed, but thou
Art pining in a dungeon now,
  Where thou must ever be;

No voice but mine can reach thine ear,
And Heaven has kindly sent me here,
  To mourn and sigh with thee,
And tell thee of the cherished land
  Of thy nativity.'

Blow on, wild wind, thy solemn voice,
  However sad and drear,
Is nothing to the gloomy silence
  I have had to bear.

Hot tears are streaming from my eyes,
  But these are better far
Than that dull gnawing tearless time
  The stupor of despair.

Confined and hopeless as I am,
  Oh, speak of liberty,
Oh, tell me of my mountain home,
  And I will welcome thee.

THE PARTING

I

The chestnut steed stood by the gate
His noble master's will to wait,
The woody park so green and bright
Was glowing in the morning light,
The young leaves of the aspen trees
Were dancing in the morning breeze.
The palace door was open wide,
  The lord was standing there,

And his sweet lady by his side
  With soft dark eyes and raven hair.
He smiling took her wary hand
And said, 'No longer here I stand;
My charger shakes his flowing mane
And calls me with impatient neigh.
Adieu then till we meet again,
Sweet love, I must no longer stay.'

'You must not go so soon,' she said,
  'I will not say farewell.
The sun has not dispelled the shade
  In yonder dewy dell;
Dark shadows of gigantic length
  Are sleeping on the lawn;
And scarcely have the birds begun
  To hail the summer morn;
Then stay with me a little while,'
She said with soft and sunny smile.

He smiled again and did not speak,
But lightly kissed her rosy cheek,
And fondly claspéd her in his arms,
  Then vaulted on his steed.
And down the park's smooth winding road
  He urged its flying speed.
Still by the door his lady stood
  And watched his rapid flight,
Until he came to a distant wood
  That hid him from her sight.
But ere he vanished from her view
He waved to her a last adieu,
Then onward hastily he steered
And in the forest disappeared.

The lady smiled a pensive smile
  And heaved a gently sigh,
But her cheek was all unbleached the while
  And tearless was her eye.
'A thousand lovely flowers,' she said,
  'Are smiling on the plain.
And ere one half of them are dead,
  My lord will come again.
The leaves are waving fresh and green
  On every stately tree,
And long before they die away

He will return to me!'—
Alas! Fair lady, say not so;
Thou canst not tell the weight of woe
   That lies in store for thee.

Those flowers will fade, those leaves will fall,
Winter will darken yonder hall;
Sweet spring will smile o'er hill and plain
And trees and flowers will bloom again,
And years will still keep rolling on,
But thy belovéd lord is gone.
His absence thou shalt deeply mourn,
And never smile on his return.

THE PARTING

II

The lady of Abyerno's hall
   Is waiting for her lord;
The blackbird's song, the cuckoo's call
   No joy to her afford.
She smiles not at the summer's sun,
   Nor at the winter's blast;
She mourns that she is still alone
   Though three long years have passed.

I knew her when her eye was bright,
I knew her when her step was light
And blithesome as a mountain doe's,
And when her cheek was like the rose,
And when her voice was full and free,
And when her smile was sweet to see.

But now the lustre of her eye,
   Is dimmed with many a tear;
Her footstep's elasticity,
   Is timed with grief and fear;
The rose has left her hollow cheeks;
In low and mournful tone she speaks,
And when she smiles 'tis but a gleam
   Of sunshine on a winter's day,
That faintly beams through dreary clouds,
   And in a moment dies away.
It does not warm, it does not cheer,
   It makes us sigh for summer days
When fields are green, and skies are clear,
   And when the sun has kinder rays.

For three years she has waited there,
   Still hoping for her lord's return,
But vainly she may hope and fear
   And vainly watch and weep and mourn;
She may wait him till her hairs are grey,
And she may wear her life away,
But to his lady and his home
Her noble lord will never come.

'I wish I knew the worst,' she said,
   'I wish I could despair.
These fruitless hopes, this constant dread,
   Are more than I can bear!'

'Then do not hope and do not weep,
   He loved thee faithfully,
And nothing short of death could keep
   So true a heart from thee;
Eliza, he would never go,
   And leave thee thus to mourn,
He must be dead, for death alone
   Could hinder his return.'

'Twas thus I spoke because I felt
   As if my heart would break,
To see her thus so slowly pining
   For Abyerno's sake.
But more than that I would not tell,
Though all the while I knew so well
The time and nature of his death.
For when he drew his parting breath
His head was pillowed on my knee,
And his dark eyes were turned to me
With and agonised heart-breaking glance,
   Until they saw me not
Oh, the look of a dying man
   Can never be forgot!

VERSES TO A CHILD

Oh, raise those eyes to me again
   And smile again so joyously,
And fear not, love; it was not pain
   Nor grief that drew these tears from me;
Belovéd child, thou canst not tell
The thoughts that in my bosom dwell
   Whene'er I look on thee!

Thou knowest not that a glance of thine
   Can bring back long departed years
And that thy blue eyes' magic shine
   Can overflow my own with tears,
And that each feature soft and fair
And every curl of golden hair,
   Some sweet remembrance bears.

Just then thou didst recall to me
   A distant long forgotten scene,
One smile, and one sweet word from thee
   Dispelled the years that rolled between;
I was a little child again,
And every after joy and pain
   Seemed never to have been.

Tall forest trees waved over me,
   To hide me from the heat of day,
And by my side a child like thee
   Among the summer flowerets lay.
He was thy sire, thou merry child.
Like thee he spoke, like thee he smiled,
   Like thee he used to play.

Oh, those were calm and happy days,
   We loved each other fondly then;
But human love too soon decays,
   And ours can never bloom again.
I never thought to see the day
When Florian's friendship would decay
   Like those of colder men.

Now, Flora, thou hast but begun
   To sail on life's deceitful sea,
Oh, do not err as I have done,
   For I have trusted foolishly;
The faith of every friend I loved
I never doubted till I proved
   Their heart's inconstancy.

'Tis mournful to look back upon
   Those long departed joys and cares,
But I *will* weep since thou alone
   Art witness to my streaming tears.
This lingering love will not depart,
I cannot banish from my heart
   The friend of childish years.

But though thy father loves me not,
   Yet I shall still be loved by thee,
And though I am by him forgot,
   Say wilt thou not remember me!
I will not cause *thy* heart to ache;
For thy regretted father's sake
   I'll love and cherish thee.

SELF-CONGRATULATION

Ellen, you were thoughtless once
   Of beauty or of grace,
Simple and homely in attire,
   Careless of form and face;
Then whence this change? and wherefore now
   So often smoothe your hair?
And wherefore deck your youthful form
   With such unwearied care?

Tell us, and cease to tire our ears
   With that familiar strain;
Why will you play those simple tunes
   So often o'er again?
"Indeed, dear friends, I can but say
   That childhood's thoughts are gone;
Each year its own new feelings brings,
   And years move swiftly on:

"And for these little simple airs—
   I love to play them o'er
So much—I dare not promise, now,
   To play them never more."
I answered—and it was enough;
   They turned them to depart;
They could not read my secret thoughts,
   Nor see my throbbing heart.

I've noticed many a youthful form,
   Upon whose changeful face
The inmost workings of the soul
   The gazer well might trace;
The speaking eye, the changing lip,
   The ready blushing cheek,
The smiling, or beclouded brow,
   Their different feelings speak.

But, thank God! you might gaze on mine
  For hours, and never know
The secret changes of my soul
  From joy to keenest woe.
Last night, as we sat round the fire
  Conversing merrily,
We heard, without, approaching steps
  Of one well known to me!

There was no trembling in my voice,
  No blush upon my cheek,
No lustrous sparkle in my eyes,
  Of hope, or joy, to speak;
But, oh! my spirit burned within,
  My heart beat full and fast!
He came not nigh—he went away—
  And then my joy was past.

And yet my comrades marked it not:
  My voice was still the same;
They saw me smile, and o'er my face
  No signs of sadness came.
They little knew my hidden thoughts;
  And they will *never* know
The aching anguish of my heart,
  The bitter burning woe!

THE BLUEBELL

A fine and subtle spirit dwells
  In every little flower,
Each one its own sweet feeling breathes
  With more or less of power.

There is a silent eloquence
  In every wild bluebell
That fills my softened heart with bliss
  That words could never tell.

Yet I recall not long ago
  A bright and sunny day,
'Twas when I led a toilsome life
  So many leagues away;

That day along a sunny road
   All carelessly I strayed,
Between two banks where smiling flowers
   Their varied hues displayed.

Before me rose a lofty hill,
   Behind me lay the sea,
My heart was not so heavy then
   As it was wont to be.

Less harassed than at other times
   I saw the scene was fair,
And spoke and laughed to those around,
   As if I knew no care.

But when I looked upon the bank
   My wandering glances fell
Upon a little trembling flower,
   A single sweet bluebell.

Whence came that rising in my throat,
   That dimness in my eye?
Why did those burning drops distil—
   Those bitter feelings rise?

Oh, that lone flower recalled to me
   My happy childhood's hours
When bluebells seemed like fairy gifts
   A prize among the flowers,

Those sunny days of merriment
   When heart and soul were free,
And when I dwelt with kindred hearts
   That loved and cared for me.

I had not then mid heartless crowds
   To spend a thankless life
In seeking after others' weal
   With anxious toil and strife.

'Sad wanderer, weep those blissful times
   That never may return!'
The lovely floweret seemed to say,
   And thus it made me mourn.

AN ORPHAN'S LAMENT

She's gone—and twice the summer's sun
  Has gilt Regina's towers,
And melted wild Angora's snows,
  And warmed Epina's bowers.

The flowerets twice on hill and dale
  Have bloomed and died away,
And twice the rustling forest leaves
  Have fallen to decay,

And thrice stern winter's icy hand
  Has checked the river's flow,
And three times o'er the mountains thrown
  His spotless robe of snow.

Two summers springs and autumns sad
  Three winters cold and grey—
And is it then so long ago
  That wild November day!

They say such tears as children weep
  Will soon be dried away,
That childish grief however strong
  Is only for a day,

And parted friends how dear soe'er
  Will soon forgotten be;
It may be so with other hearts,
  It is not thus with me.

My mother, thou wilt weep no more
  For thou art gone above,
But can I ever cease to mourn
  Thy good and fervent love?

While that was mine the world to me
  Was sunshine bright and fair;
No feeling rose within my heart
  But thou couldst read it there.

And thou couldst feel for all my joys
  And all my childish cares
And never weary of my play
  Or scorn my foolish fears.

Beneath thy sweet maternal smile
　All pain and sorrow fled,
And even the very tears were sweet
　Upon thy bosom shed.

Thy loss can never be repaired;
　I shall not know again
While life remains, the peaceful joy
　That filled my spirit then.

Where shall I find a heart like thine
　While life remains to me,
And where shall I bestow the love
　I ever bore for thee?

LINES WRITTEN AT THORP GREEN

That summer sun, whose genial glow
Now cheers my drooping spirit so
　Must cold and distant be,
And only light our northern clime
With feeble ray, before the time
　I long so much to see.

And this soft whispering breeze that now
So gently cools my fevered brow,
　This too, alas, must turn—
To a wild blast whose icy dart
Pierces and chills me to the heart,
　Before I cease to mourn.

And these bright flowers I love so well,
Verbena, rose and sweet bluebell,
　Must droop and die away.
Those thick green leaves with all their shade
And rustling music, they must fade
　And every one decay.

But if the sunny summer time
And woods and meadows in their prime
　Are sweet to them that roam—
Far sweeter is the winter bare
With long dark nights and landscapes drear
　To them that are at Home!

APPEAL

Oh, I am very weary,
  Though tears no longer flow;
My eyes are tired of weeping,
  My heart is sick of woe;

My life is very lonely
  My days pass heavily,
I'm weary of repining;
  Wilt thou not come to me?

Oh, didst thou know my longings
  For thee, from day to day,
My hopes, so often blighted,
  Thou wouldst not thus delay!

DESPONDENCY

I have gone backward in the work;
  The labour has not sped;
Drowsy and dark my spirit lies,
  Heavy and dull as lead.

How can I rouse my sinking soul
  From such a lethargy?
How can I break these iron chains
  And set my spirit free?

There have been times when I have mourned!
  In anguish o'er the past,
And raised my suppliant hands on high,
  While tears fell thick and fast;

And prayed to have my sins forgiven,
  With such a fervent zeal,
An earnest grief, a strong desire
  As now I cannot feel.

And I have felt so full of love,
  So strong in spirit then,
As if my heart would never cool,
  Or wander back again.

And yet, alas! how many times
  My feet have gone astray!
How oft have I forgot my God!
  How greatly fallen away!

My sins increase—my love grows cold,
  And Hope within me dies:
Even Faith itself is wavering now;
  Oh, how shall I arise?

I cannot weep, but I can pray,
  Then let me not despair:
Lord Jesus, save me, lest I die!
  Christ, hear my humble prayer!

TO COWPER

Sweet are thy strains, celestial Bard;
  And oft, in childhood's years,
I've read them o'er and o'er again,
  With floods of silent tears.

The language of my inmost heart
  I traced in every line;
My sins, *my* sorrows, hopes, and fears,
  Were there-and only mine.

All for myself the sigh would swell,
  The tear of anguish start;
I little knew what wilder woe
  Had filled the Poet's heart.

I did not know the nights of gloom,
  The days of misery;
The long, long years of dark despair,
  That crushed and tortured thee.

But they are gone; from earth at length
  Thy gentle soul is pass'd,
And in the bosom of its God
  Has found its home at last.

It must be so, if God is love,
  And answers fervent prayer;
Then surely thou shalt dwell on high,
  And I may meet thee there.

Is He the source of every good,
   The spring of purity?
Then in thine hours of deepest woe,
   Thy God was still with thee.

How else, when every hope was fled,
   Couldst thou so fondly cling
To holy things and help men?
   And how so sweetly sing,

Of things that God alone could teach?
   And whence that purity,
That hatred of all sinful ways—
   That gentle charity?

Are *these* the symptoms of a heart
   Of heavenly grace bereft—
For ever banished from its God,
   To Satan's fury left?

Yet, should thy darkest fears be true,
   If Heaven be so severe,
That such a soul as thine is lost,—
   Oh! how shall *I* appear?

IN MEMORY OF A HAPPY DAY IN FEBRUARY

Blessed be Thou for all the joy
   My soul has felt to-day!
Oh, let its memory stay with me,
   And never pass away!

I was alone, for those I loved
   Were far away from me;
The sun shone on the withered grass,
   The wind blew fresh and free.

Was it the smile of early spring
   That made my bosom glow?
'Twas sweet; but neither sun nor wind
   Could cheer my spirit so.

Was it some feeling of delight
   All vague and undefined?
No; 'twas a rapture deep and strong,
   Expanding in the mind.

Was it a sanguine view of life,
   And all its transient bliss,
A hope of bright prosperity?
   Oh, no! it was not this.

It was a glimpse of truth divine
   Unto my spirit given,
Illumined by a ray of light
   That shone direct from heaven.

I felt there was a God on high,
   By whom all things were made;
I saw His wisdom and His power
   In all his works displayed.

But most throughout the moral world,
   I saw his glory shine;
I saw His wisdom infinite,
   His mercy all divine.

Deep secrets of His providence,
   In darkness long concealed,
Unto the vision of my soul
   Were graciously revealed.

But while I wondered and adored
   His Majesty divine,
I did not tremble at His power:
   I felt that God was mine;

I knew that my Redeemer lived;
   I did not fear to die;
Full sure that I should rise again
   To immortality.

I longed to view that bliss divine,
   Which eye hath never seen;
Like Moses, I would see His face
   Without the veil between.

LINES COMPOSED IN A WOOD ON A WINDY DAY

My soul is awakened, my spirit is soaring
   And carried aloft on the wings of the breeze;
For above and around me the wild wind is roaring,
   Arousing to rapture the earth and the seas.

The long withered grass in the sunshine is glancing,
　　The bare trees are tossing their branches on high;
The dead leaves beneath them are merrily dancing,
　　The white clouds are scudding across the blue sky

I wish I could see how the ocean is lashing
　　The foam of its billows to whirlwinds of spray;
I wish I could see how its proud waves are dashing,
　　And hear the wild roar of their thunder to-day!

A WORD TO THE 'ELECT.'

You may rejoice to think *yourselves* secure;
You may be grateful for the gift divine—
That grace unsought, which made your black hearts pure,
And fits your earth-born souls in Heaven to shine.

But, is it sweet to look around, and view
Thousands excluded from that happiness
Which they deserved, at least, as much as you.—
Their faults not greater, nor their virtues less?

And wherefore should you love your God the more,
Because to you alone his smiles are given;
Because He chose to pass the *many* o'er,
And only bring the favoured *few* to Heaven?

And, wherefore should your hearts more grateful prove,
Because for *all* the Saviour did not die?
Is yours the God of justice and of love?
And are your bosoms warm with charity?

Say, does your heart expand to all mankind?
And, would you ever to your neighbour do—
The weak, the strong, the enlightened, and the blind—
As you would have your neighbour do to you?

And when you, looking on your fellow-men,
Behold them doomed to endless misery,
How can you talk of joy and rapture then?—
May God withhold such cruel joy from me!

That none deserve eternal bliss I know;
Unmerited the grace in mercy given:
But, none shall sink to everlasting woe,
That have not well deserved the wrath of Heaven.

And, oh! there lives within my heart
   A hope, long nursed by me;
(And should its cheering ray depart,
   How dark my soul would be!)

That as in Adam all have died,
   In Christ shall all men live;
And ever round his throne abide,
   Eternal praise to give.

That even the wicked shall at last
   Be fitted for the skies;
And when their dreadful doom is past,
   To life and light arise.

I ask not, how remote the day,
   Nor what the sinners' woe,
Before their dross is purged away;
   Enough for me to know—

That when the clip of wrath is drained,
   The metal purified,
They'll cling to what they once disdained,
   And live by Him that died.

THE DOUBTER'S PRAYER

Eternal Power, of earth and air!
Unseen, yet seen in all around,
Remote, but dwelling everywhere,
Though silent, heard in every sound;

If e'er thine ear in mercy bent,
When wretched mortals cried to Thee,
And if, indeed, Thy Son was sent,
To save lost sinners such as me:

Then hear me now, while kneeling here,
I lift to thee my heart and eye,
And all my soul ascends in prayer,
Oh, give me—give me Faith! I cry.

Without some glimmering in my heart,
I could not raise this fervent prayer;
But, oh! a stronger light impart,
And in Thy mercy fix it there.

While Faith is with me, I am blest;
It turns my darkest night to day;
But while I clasp it to my breast,
I often feel it slide away.

Then, cold and dark, my spirit sinks,
To see my light of life depart;
And every fiend of Hell, methinks,
Enjoys the anguish of my heart.

What shall I do, if all my love,
My hopes, my toil, are cast away,
And if there be no God above,
To hear and bless me when I pray?

If this be vain delusion all,
If death be an eternal sleep,
And none can hear my secret call,
Or see the silent tears I weep!

Oh, help me, God! For thou alone
Canst my distracted soul relieve;
Forsake it not: it is thine own,
Though weak, yet longing to believe.

Oh, drive these cruel doubts away;
And make me know, that Thou art God!
A faith, that shines by night and day,
Will lighten every earthly load.

If I believe that Jesus died,
And waking, rose to reign above;
Then surely Sorrow, Sin, and Pride,
Must yield to Peace, and Hope, and Love.

And all the blessed words He said
Will strength and holy joy impart:
A shield of safety o'er my head,
A spring of comfort in my heart.

THE CAPTIVE DOVE

Poor restless dove, I pity thee;
And when I hear thy plaintive moan,
I mourn for thy captivity,
And in thy woes forget mine own.

To see thee stand prepared to fly,
And flap those useless wings of thine,
And gaze into the distant sky,
Would melt a harder heart than mine.

In vain—in vain! Thou canst not rise:
Thy prison roof confines thee there;
Its slender wires delude thine eyes,
And quench thy longings with despair.

Oh, thou wert made to wander free
In sunny mead and shady grove,
And far beyond the rolling sea,
In distant climes, at will to rove!

Yet, hadst thou but one gentle mate
Thy little drooping heart to cheer,
And share with thee thy captive state,
Thou couldst be happy even there.

Yes, even there, if, listening by,
One faithful dear companion stood,
While gazing on her full bright eye,
Thou mightst forget thy native wood

But thou, poor solitary dove,
Must make, unheard, thy joyless moan;
The heart that Nature formed to love
Must pine, neglected, and alone.

THE CONSOLATION

Though bleak these woods, and damp the ground
    With fallen leaves so thickly strown,
And cold the wind that wanders round
    With wild and melancholy moan;

There *is* a friendly roof, I know,
    Might shield me from the wintry blast;
There is a fire, whose ruddy glow
    Will cheer me for my wanderings past.

And so, though still, where'er I go,
    Cold stranger-glances meet my eye;
Though, when my spirit sinks in woe,
    Unheeded swells the unbidden sigh;

Though solitude, endured too long,
  Bids youthful joys too soon decay,
Makes mirth a stranger to my tongue,
  And overclouds my noon of day;

When kindly thoughts that would have way,
  Flow back discouraged to my breast;
I know there is, though far away,
  A home where heart and soul may rest.

Warm hands are there, that, claspéd in mine,
  The warmer heart will not belie;
While mirth, and truth, and friendship shine
  In smiling lip and earnest eye.

The ice that gathers round my heart
  May there be thawed; and sweetly, then,
The joys of youth, that now depart,
  Will come to cheer my soul again.

Though far I roam, that thought shall be
  My hope, my comfort, everywhere;
While such a home remains to me,
  My heart shall never know despair!

PAST DAYS

'Tis strange to think there *was* a time
When mirth was not an empty name,
When laughter really cheered the heart,
And frequent smiles unbidden came,
And tears of grief would only flow
In sympathy for others' woe;

When speech expressed the inward thought,
And heart to kindred heart was bare,
And summer days were far too short
For all the pleasures crowded there;
And silence, solitude, and rest,
Now welcome to the weary breast—

Were all unprized, uncourted then—
And all the joy one spirit showed,
The other deeply felt again;
And friendship like a river flowed,
Constant and strong its silent course,
For nought withstood its gentle force:

When night, the holy time of peace,
Was dreaded as the parting hour;
When speech and mirth at once must cease,
And silence must resume her power;
Though ever free from pains and woes,
She only brought us calm repose.

And when the blessed dawn again
Brought daylight to the blushing skies,
We woke, and not *reluctant* then,
To joyless *labour* did we rise;
But full of hope, and glad and gay,
We welcomed the returning day.

THE STUDENT'S SERENADE

I have slept upon my couch,
But my spirit did not rest,
For the labours of the day
Yet my weary soul opprest;

And before my dreaming eyes
Still the learned volumes lay,
And I could not close their leaves,
And I could not turn away.

But I oped my eyes at last,
And I heard a muffled sound;
'Twas the night-breeze, come to say
That the snow was on the ground.

Then I knew that there was rest
On the mountain's bosom free;
So I left my fevered couch,
And I flew to waken thee!

I have flown to waken thee—
For, if thou wilt not arise,
Then my soul can drink no peace
From these holy moonlight skies.

And this waste of virgin snow
To my sight will not be fair,
Unless thou wilt smiling come,
Love, to wander with me there.

Then, awake! Maria, wake!
For, if thou couldst only know
How the quiet moonlight sleeps
On this wilderness of snow,

And the groves of ancient trees,
In their snowy garb arrayed,
Till they stretch into the gloom
Of the distant valley's shade;

I know thou wouldst rejoice
To inhale this bracing air;
Thou wouldst break thy sweetest sleep
To behold a scene so fair.

O'er these wintry wilds, *alone*,
Thou wouldst joy to wander free;
And it will not please thee less,
Though that bliss be shared with me.

A REMINISCENCE

Yes, thou art gone! and never more
Thy sunny smile shall gladden me;
But I may pass the old church door,
And pace the floor that covers thee,

May stand upon the cold, damp stone,
And think that, frozen, lies below
The lightest heart that I have known,
The kindest I shall ever know.

Yet, though I cannot see thee more,
'Tis still a comfort to have seen;
And though thy transient life is o'er,
'Tis sweet to think that thou hast been;

To think a soul so near divine,
Within a form so angel fair,
United to a heart like thine,
Has gladdened once our humble sphere.

MEMORY

Brightly the sun of summer shone
Green fields and waving woods upon,
   And soft winds wandered by;
Above, a sky of purest blue,
Around, bright flowers of loveliest hue,
   Allured the gazer's eye.

But what were all these charms to me,
When one sweet breath of memory
   Came gently wafting by?
I closed my eyes against the day,
And called my willing soul away,
   From earth, and air, and sky;

That I might simply fancy there
One little flower—a primrose fair,
   Just opening into sight;
As in the days of infancy,
An opening primrose seemed to me
   A source of strange delight.

Sweet Memory! ever smile on me;
Nature's chief beauties spring from thee;
   Oh, still thy tribute bring
Still make the golden crocus shine
Among the flowers the most divine,
   The glory of the spring.

Still in the wallflower's fragrance dwell;
And hover round the slight bluebell,
   My childhood's darling flower.
Smile on the little daisy still,
The buttercup's bright goblet fill
   With all thy former power.

For ever hang thy dreamy spell
Round mountain star and heather bell,
   And do not pass away
From sparkling frost, or wreathed snow,
And whisper when the wild winds blow,
   Or rippling waters play.

Is childhood, then, so all divine?
Or Memory, is the glory thine,
   That haloes thus the past?
Not *all* divine; its pangs of grief
(Although, perchance, their stay be brief)
   Are bitter while they last.

Nor is the glory all thine own,
For on our earliest joys alone
   That holy light is cast.
With such a ray, no spell of thine
Can make our later pleasures shine,
   Though long ago they passed.

FLUCTUATIONS

What though the Sun had left my sky;
   To save me from despair
The blessed Moon arose on high,
   And shone serenely there.

I watched her, with a tearful gaze,
   Rise slowly o'er the hill,
While through the dim horizon's haze
   Her light gleamed faint and chill.

I thought such wan and lifeless beams
   Could ne'er my heart repay
For the bright sun's most transient gleams
   That cheered me through the day:

But, as above that mist's control
   She rose, and brighter shone,
I felt her light upon my soul;
   But now—that light is gone!

Thick vapours snatched her from my sight,
   And I was darkling left,
All in the cold and gloomy night,
   Of light and hope bereft:

Until, methought, a little star
   Shone forth with trembling ray,
To cheer me with its light afar—
   But that, too, passed away.

Anon, an earthly meteor blazed
   The gloomy darkness through;
I smiled, yet trembled while I gazed—
   But that soon vanished too!

And darker, drearier fell the night
   Upon my spirit then;—
But what is that faint struggling light?
   Is it the Moon again?

Kind Heaven! increase that silvery gleam
   And bid these clouds depart,
And let her soft celestial beam
   Restore my fainting heart!

A PRAYER

My God (oh, let me call Thee mine,
   Weak, wretched sinner though I be),
My trembling soul would fain be Thine;
   My feeble faith still clings to Thee.

Not only for the Past I grieve,
   The Future fills me with dismay;
Unless Thou hasten to relieve,
   Thy suppliant is a castaway.

I cannot say my faith is strong,
   I dare not hope my love is great;
But strength and love to Thee belong;
   Oh, do not leave me desolate!

I know I owe my all to Thee;
   Oh, *take* the heart I cannot give!
Do Thou my strength—my Saviour be,
   And *make* me to Thy glory live.

THE DUNGEON

Though not a breath can enter here,
   I know the wind blows fresh and free;
I know the sun is shining clear,
   Though not a gleam can visit me.

They thought while I in darkness lay,
   'Twere pity that I should not know
How all the earth is smiling gay;
   How fresh the vernal breezes blow.

They knew, such tidings to impart
   Would pierce my weary spirit through,
And could they better read my heart,
   They'd tell me, *she* was smiling too.

They need not, for I know it well,
   Methinks I see her even now;
No sigh disturbs her bosom's swell,
   No shade o'ercasts her angel brow.

Unmarred by grief her angel voice,
   Whence sparkling wit, and wisdom flow:
And others in its sound rejoice,
   And taste the joys I must not know,

Drink rapture from her soft dark eye,
   And sunshine from her heavenly smile;
On wings of bliss their moments fly,
   And I am pining here the while!

Oh! tell me, does she never give—
   To my distress a single sigh?
She smiles on them, but does she grieve
   One moment, when they are not by?

When she beholds the sunny skies,
   And feels the wind of heaven blow;
Has she no tear for him that lies
   In dungeon gloom, so far below?

While others gladly round her press
   And at her side their hours beguile,
Has she no sigh for his distress
   Who cannot see a single smile

Nor hear one word nor read a line
   That her belovéd hand might write,
Who banished from her face must pine
   Each day a long and lonely night?

HOME

How brightly glistening in the sun
  The woodland ivy plays!
While yonder beeches from their barks
  Reflect his silver rays.

That sun surveys a lovely scene
  From softly smiling skies;
And wildly through unnumbered trees
  The wind of winter sighs:

Now loud, it thunders o'er my head,
  And now in distance dies.
But give me back my barren hills
  Where colder breezes rise;

Where scarce the scattered, stunted trees
  Can yield an answering swell,
But where a wilderness of heath
  Returns the sound as well.

For yonder garden, fair and wide,
  With groves of evergreen,
Long winding walks, and borders trim,
  And velvet lawns between;

Restore to me that little spot,
  With gray walls compassed round,
Where knotted grass neglected lies,
  And weeds usurp the ground.

Though all around this mansion high
  Invites the foot to roam,
And though its halls are fair within—
  Oh, give me back my *home*!

CALL ME AWAY

Call me away; there's nothing here,
  That wins my soul to stay;
Then let me leave this prospect drear,
  And hasten far away.

To our belovéd land I'll flee,
   Our land of thought and soul,
Where I have roved so oft with thee,
   Beyond the world's control.

I'll sit and watch those ancient trees,
   Those Scotch firs dark and high;
I'll listen to the eerie breeze,
   Among their branches sigh.

The glorious moon shines far above;
   How soft her radiance falls,
On snowy heights, and rock, and grove;
   And yonder palace walls!

Who stands beneath yon fir trees high?
   A youth both slight and fair,
Whose bright and restless azure eye
   Proclaims him known to care,

Though fair that brow, it is not smooth;
   Dark lines spread 'neath the hair;
Though small those features, yet in sooth
   Stern passion has been there.

Now on the peaceful moon are fixed
   Those eyes so glistening bright,
But trembling teardrops hang betwixt,
   And dim the blessed light.

Though late the hour, and keen the blast,
   That whistles round him now,
Those raven locks are backward cast,
   To cool his burning brow.

His hands above his heaving breast
   Are claspéd in agony—
'Oh, Father! Father! let me rest!
   And call my soul to thee!

'I know 'tis weakness thus to pray;
   But all this cankering care—
This doubt tormenting night and day
   Is more than I can bear!

'With none to comfort, none to guide
   And none to strengthen me.
Since thou my only friend hast died—
   I've pined to follow thee!
Since thou hast died! And did he live
'What comfort could his counsel give—
   To one forlorn like me?

'Would *he* my Idol's form adore—
   Her soul, her glance, her tone?
And say, "Forget for ever more
   Her kindred and thine own;
Let dreams of her thy peace destroy,
Leave every other hope and joy
   And live for her alone"?'

He starts, he smiles, and dries the tears,
   Still glistening on his cheek,
The lady of his soul appears,
   And hark! I hear her speak—

'Aye, dry thy tears; thou wilt not weep—
   While I am by thy side—
Our foes all day their watch may keep
   But cannot thus divide

'Such hearts as ours; and we tonight
   Their malice will deride,
Together in the clear moon's light
   Their malice will deride.

'No fear our present bliss shall blast
   And sorrow we'll defy.
Do thou forget the dreary past,
   The dreadful future *I*.'

'Forget it? Yes, while thou art by
   I think of nought but thee,
'Tis only when thou art not nigh
   Remembrance tortures me.

'But such a lofty soul to find,
　　And such a heart as thine,
In such a glorious form enshrined
　　And still to call thee mine—
Would be for earth too great a bliss,
Without a taint of woe like this,
　　Then why should I repine?

NIGHT

I love the silent hour of night,
　　For blissful dreams may then arise,
Revealing to my charmèd sight
　　What may not bless my waking eyes!

And then a voice may meet my ear
　　That death has silenced long ago;
And hope and rapture may appear
　　Instead of solitude and woe.

Cold in the grave for years has lain
　　The form it was my bliss to see,
And only dreams can bring again
　　The darling of my heart to me.

DREAMS

While on my lonely couch I lie,
　　I seldom feel myself alone,
For fancy fills my dreaming eye
　　With scenes and pleasures of its own.

Then I may cherish at my breast
　　An infant's form belovéd and fair,
May smile and soothe it into rest
　　With all a Mother's fondest care.

How sweet to feel its helpless form
　　Depending thus on me alone!
And while I hold it safe and warm
　　What bliss to think it is my own!

And glances then may meet my eyes
　　That daylight never showed to me;
What raptures in my bosom rise,
　　Those earnest looks of love to see,

To feel my hand so kindly prest,
   To know myself belovéd at last,
To think my heart has found a rest,
   My life of solitude is past!

But then to wake and find it flown,
   The dream of happiness destroyed,
To find myself unloved, alone,
   What tongue can speak the dreary void?

A heart whence warm affections flow,
   Creator, thou hast given to me,
And am I only thus to know
   How sweet the joys of love would be?

IF THIS BE ALL

Oh, God! if this indeed be all
   That Life can show to me;
If on my aching brow may fall
   No freshening dew from Thee;

If with no brighter light than this
   The lamp of hope may glow,
And I may only *dream* of bliss,
   And wake to weary woe;

If friendship's solace must decay,
   When other joys are gone,
And love must keep so far away,
   While I go wandering on,—

Wandering and toiling without gain,
   The slave of others' will,
With constant care, and frequent pain,
   Despised, forgotten still;

Grieving to look on vice and sin,
   Yet powerless to quell
The silent current from within,
   The outward torrent's swell

While all the good I would impart,
   The feelings I would share,
Are driven backward to my heart,
   And turned to wormwood there;

If clouds must *ever* keep from sight
 The glories of the Sun,
And I must suffer Winter's blight,
 Ere Summer is begun;

If Life must be so full of care,
 Then call me soon to thee;
Or give me strength enough to bear
 My load of misery.

CONFIDENCE

Oppressed with sin and woe,
 A burdened heart I bear,
Opposed by many a mighty foe;
 But I will not despair.

With this polluted heart,
 I dare to come to Thee,
Holy and mighty as Thou art,
 For Thou wilt pardon me.

I feel that I am weak,
 And prone to every sin;
But Thou who giv'st to those who seek,
 Wilt give me strength within.

Far as this earth may be
 From yonder starry skies;
Remoter still am I from Thee:
 Yet Thou wilt not despise.

I need not fear my foes,
 I deed not yield to care;
I need not sink beneath my woes,
 For Thou wilt answer prayer.

In my Redeemer's name,
 I give myself to Thee;
And, all unworthy as I am,
 My God will cherish me.

VIEWS OF LIFE

When sinks my heart in hopeless gloom,
And life can show no joy for me;
And I behold a yawning tomb,
Where bowers and palaces should be;

In vain you talk of morbid dreams;
In vain you gaily smiling say,
That what to me so dreary seems,
The healthy mind deems bright and gay.

I too have smiled, and thought like you,
But madly smiled, and falsely deemed:
Truth led me to the present view,—
I'm waking now—'twas *then* I dreamed.

I lately saw a sunset sky,
And stood enraptured to behold
Its varied hues of glorious dye:
First, fleecy clouds of shining gold;

These blushing took a rosy hue;
Beneath them shone a flood of green;
Nor less divine, the glorious blue
That smiled above them and between.

I cannot name each lovely shade;
I cannot say how bright they shone;
But one by one, I saw them fade;
And what remained when they were gone?

Dull clouds remained, of sombre hue,
And when their borrowed charm was o'er,
The azure sky had faded too,
That smiled so softly bright before.

So, gilded by the glow of youth,
Our varied life looks fair and gay;
And so remains the naked truth,
When that false light is past away.

Why blame ye, then, my keener sight,
That clearly sees a world of woes
Through all the haze of golden light
That flattering Falsehood round it throws?

When the young mother smiles above
The first-born darling of her heart,
Her bosom glows with earnest love,
While tears of silent transport start.

Fond dreamer! little does she know
The anxious toil, the suffering,
The blasted hopes, the burning woe,
The object of her joy will bring.

Her blinded eyes behold not now
What, soon or late, must be his doom;
The anguish that will cloud his brow,
The bed of death, the dreary tomb.

As little know the youthful pair,
In mutual love supremely blest,
What weariness, and cold despair,
Ere long, will seize the aching breast.

And even should Love and Faith remain,
(The greatest blessings life can show,)
Amid adversity and pain,
To shine throughout with cheering glow;

They do not see how cruel Death
Comes on, their loving hearts to part:
One feels not now the gasping breath,
The rending of the earth-bound heart,—

The soul's and body's agony,
Ere she may sink to her repose.
The sad survivor cannot see
The grave above his darling close;

Nor how, despairing and alone,
He then must wear his life away;
And linger, feebly toiling on,
And fainting, sink into decay.

* * * *

Oh, Youth may listen patiently,
While sad Experience tells her tale,
But Doubt sits smiling in his eye,
For ardent Hope will still prevail!

He hears how feeble Pleasure dies,
By guilt destroyed, and pain and woe;
He turns to Hope—and she replies,
"Believe it not-it is not so!"

"Oh, heed her not!" Experience says;
"For thus she whispered once to me;
She told me, in my youthful days,
How glorious manhood's prime would be.

"When, in the time of early Spring,
Too chill the winds that o'er me pass'd,
She said, each coming day would bring
A fairer heaven, a gentler blast.

"And when the sun too seldom beamed,
The sky, o'ercast, too darkly frowned,
The soaking rain too constant streamed,
And mists too dreary gathered round;

"She told me, Summer's glorious ray
Would chase those vapours all away,
    And scatter glories round;
With sweetest music fill the trees,
Load with rich scent the gentle breeze,
    And strew with flowers the ground

"But when, beneath that scorching ray,
I languished, weary through the day,
    While birds refused to sing,
Verdure decayed from field and tree,
And panting Nature mourned with me
    The freshness of the Spring.

"'Wait but a little while,' she said,
'Till Summer's burning days are fled;
    And Autumn shall restore,
With golden riches of her own,
And Summer's glories mellowed down,
    The freshness you deplore.'

And long I waited, but in vain:
That freshness never came again,
    Though Summer passed away,
Though Autumn's mists hung cold and chill.
And drooping nature languished still,
    And sank into decay.

"Till wintry blasts foreboding blew
Through leafless trees—and then I knew
   That Hope was all a dream.
But thus, fond youth, she cheated me;
And she will prove as false to thee,
   Though sweet her words may seem.

Stern prophet! Cease thy bodings dire—
Thou canst not quench the ardent fire
   That warms the breast of youth.
Oh, let it cheer him while it may,
And gently, gently die away—
   Chilled by the damps of truth!

Tell him, that earth is not our rest;
Its joys are empty—frail at best;
   And point beyond the sky.
But gleams of light may reach us here;
And hope the *roughest* path can cheer:
   Then do not bid it fly!

Though hope may promise joys, that still
Unkindly time will ne'er fulfil;
   Or, if they come at all,
We never find them unalloyed,—
Hurtful perchance, or soon destroyed,
   They vanish or they pall;

Yet hope *itself* a brightness throws
O'er all our labours and our woes;
   While dark foreboding Care
A thousand ills will oft portend,
That Providence may ne'er intend
   The trembling heart to bear.

Or if they come, it oft appears,
Our woes are lighter than our fears,
   And far more bravely borne.
Then let us not enhance our doom
But e'en in midnight's blackest gloom
   Expect the rising morn.

Because the road is rough and long,
Shall we despise the skylark's song,
   That cheers the wanderer's way?
Or trample down, with reckless feet,
The smiling flowerets, bright and sweet,
   Because they soon decay?

Pass pleasant scenes unnoticed by,
Because the next is bleak and drear;
Or not enjoy a smiling sky,
Because a tempest may be near?

No! while we journey on our way,
We'll smile on every lovely thing;
And ever, as they pass away,
To memory and hope we'll cling.

And though that awful river flows
Before us, when the journey's past,
Perchance of all the pilgrim's woes
Most dreadful—shrink not—'tis the last!

Though icy cold, and dark, and deep;
Beyond it smiles that blessed shore,
Where none shall suffer, none shall weep,
And bliss shall reign for evermore!

SONG

We know where deepest lies the snow,
And where the frost-winds keenest blow,
   O'er every mountain's brow,
We long have known and learnt to bear
The wandering outlaw's toil and care,
But where we late were hunted, there
   Our foes are hunted now.

We have their princely homes, and they
To our wild haunts are chased away,
   Dark woods, and desert caves.
And we can range from hill to hill,
And chase our vanquished victors still;
Small respite will they find until
   They slumber in their graves.

But I would rather be the hare,
That crouching in its sheltered lair
   Must start at every sound;
That forced from cornfields waving wide
Is driven to seek the bare hillside,
Or in the tangled copse to hide,
   Than be the hunter's hound.

SONG

Come to the banquet—triumph in your songs!
   Strike up the chords—and sing of Victory!
The oppressed have risen to redress their wrongs;
   The Tyrants are o'erthrown; the Land is free!
The Land is free! Aye, shout it forth once more;
Is she not red with her oppressors' gore?

We are her champions—shall we not rejoice?
   Are not the tyrants' broad domains our own?
Then wherefore triumph with a faltering voice;
   And talk of freedom in a doubtful tone?
Have we not longed through life the reign to see
Of Justice, linked with Glorious Liberty?

Shout you that will, and you that can rejoice
   To revel in the riches of your foes.
In praise of deadly vengeance lift you voice,
   Gloat o'er your tyrants' blood, you victims' woes.
I'*d* rather listen to the skylarks' songs,
And think on Gondal's, and my Father's wrongs.

It may be pleasant, to recall the death
   Of those beneath whose sheltering roof you lie;
But I would rather press the mountain heath,
   With naught to shield me from the starry sky,
And dream of yet untasted Victory—
A distant hope—and feel that I am free!

Oh, happy life! To range the mountains wild,
   The waving woods—or Ocean's heaving breast,
With limbs unfettered, conscience undefiled,
   And choosing where to wander, where to rest!
Hunted, oppressed, but ever strong to cope—
With toils, and perils—ever full of hope!

'Our flower is budding'—When that word was heard
  On desert shore, or breezy mountain's brow,
Wherever said—what glorious thoughts it stirred!
  'Twas budding then—Say has it blossomed now?
Is this the end we struggled to obtain?
Oh, for the wandering Outlaw's life again!

VANITAS VANITATUM, OMNIA VANITAS

In all we do, and hear, and see,
Is restless Toil and Vanity.
While yet the rolling earth abides,
Men come and go like ocean tides;

And ere one generation dies,
Another in its place shall rise;
That, sinking soon into the grave,
Others succeed, like wave on wave;

And as they rise, they pass away.
The sun arises every day,
And hastening onward to the West,
He nightly sinks, but not to rest:

Returning to the eastern skies,
Again to light us, he must rise.
And still the restless wind comes forth,
Now blowing keenly from the North;

Now from the South, the East, the West,
For ever changing, ne'er at rest.
The fountains, gushing from the hills,
Supply the ever-running rills;

The thirsty rivers drink their store,
And bear it rolling to the shore,
But still the ocean craves for more.
'Tis endless labour everywhere!
Sound cannot satisfy the ear,

Light cannot fill the craving eye,
Nor riches half our wants supply,
Pleasure but doubles future pain,
And joy brings sorrow in her train;

Laughter is mad, and reckless mirth—
What does she in this weary earth?
Should Wealth, or Fame, our Life employ,
Death comes, our labour to destroy;

To snatch the untasted cup away,
For which we toiled so many a day.
What, then, remains for wretched man?
To use life's comforts while he can,

Enjoy the blessings Heaven bestows,
Assist his friends, forgive his foes;
Trust God, and keep His statutes still,
Upright and firm, through good and ill;

Thankful for all that God has given,
Fixing his firmest hopes on Heaven;
Knowing that earthly joys decay,
But hoping through the darkest day.

STANZAS

Oh, weep not, love! each tear that springs
   In those dear eyes of thine,
To me a keener suffering brings
   Than if they flowed from mine.

And do not droop! however drear
   The fate awaiting thee;
For *my* sake combat pain and care,
   And cherish life for me!

I do not fear thy love will fail;
   Thy faith is true, I know;
But, oh, my love! thy strength is frail
   For such a life of woe.

Were 't not for this, I well could trace
   (Though banished long from thee)
Life's rugged path, and boldly face
   The storms that threaten me.

Fear not for me—I've steeled my mind
   Sorrow and strife to greet;
Joy with my love I leave behind,
   Care with my friends I meet.

A mother's sad reproachful eye,
  A father's scowling brow—
But he may frown and she may sigh:
  I will not break my vow!

I love my mother, I revere
  My sire, but fear not me—
Believe that Death alone can tear
  This faithful heart from thee.

THE PENITENT

I mourn with thee, and yet rejoice
  That thou shouldst sorrow so;
With angel choirs I join my voice
  To bless the sinner's woe.

Though friends and kindred turn away,
  And laugh thy grief to scorn;
I hear the great Redeemer say,
  "Blessed are ye that mourn."

Hold on thy course, nor deem it strange
  That earthly cords are riven:
Man may lament the wondrous change,
  But "there is joy in heaven!"

THE ARBOUR

I'll rest me in this sheltered bower,
And look upon the clear blue sky
That smiles upon me through the trees,
Which stand so thick clustering by;

And view their green and glossy leaves,
All glistening in the sunshine fair;
And list the rustling of their boughs,
So softly whispering through the air.

And while my ear drinks in the sound,
My winged soul shall fly away;
Reviewing lone departed years
As one mild, beaming, autumn day;

And soaring on to future scenes,
Like hills and woods, and valleys green,
All basking in the summer's sun,
But distant still, and dimly seen.

Oh, list! 'tis summer's very breath
That gently shakes the rustling trees—
But look! the snow is on the ground—
How can I think of scenes like these?

'Tis but the *frost* that clears the air,
And gives the sky that lovely blue;
They're smiling in a *winter's* sun,
Those evergreens of sombre hue.

And winter's chill is on my heart—
How can I dream of future bliss?
How can my spirit soar away,
Confined by such a chain as this?

MUSIC ON CHRISTMAS MORNING

Music I love—but never strain
Could kindle raptures so divine,
So grief assuage, so conquer pain,
And rouse this pensive heart of mine—
As that we hear on Christmas morn,
Upon the wintry breezes borne.

Though Darkness still her empire keep,
And hours must pass, ere morning break;
From troubled dreams, or slumbers deep,
That music *kindly* bids us wake:
It calls us, with an angel's voice,
To wake, and worship, and rejoice;

To greet with joy the glorious morn,
Which angels welcomed long ago,
When our redeeming Lord was born,
To bring the light of Heaven below;
The Powers of Darkness to dispel,
And rescue Earth from Death and Hell.

While listening to that sacred strain,
My raptured spirit soars on high;
I seem to hear those songs again
Resounding through the open sky,
That kindled such divine delight,
In those who watched their flocks by night.

With them I celebrate His birth—
Glory to God, in highest Heaven,
Good-will to men, and peace on earth,
To us a Saviour-king is given;
Our God is come to claim His own,
And Satan's power is overthrown!

A sinless God, for sinful men,
Descends to suffer and to bleed;
Hell *must* renounce its empire then;
The price is paid, the world is freed,
And Satan's self must now confess
That Christ has earned a *right* to bless:

Now holy Peace may smile from heaven,
And heavenly Truth from earth shall spring:
The captive's galling bonds are riven,
For our Redeemer is our king;
And He that gave his blood for men
Will lead us home to God again.

THERE LET THY BLEEDING BRANCH ATONE

There let thy bleeding branch atone
  For every torturing tear
Shall my young sins, my sins alone,
  Be everlasting here?

Who bade thee keep that cursed name
  A pledge for memory?
As if Oblivion ever came
  To breath its bliss on me;

As if, through all the wildering maze
  Of mad hours left behind,
I once forgot the early days
  That thou wouldst call to mind.

OH, THEY HAVE ROBBED ME OF THE HOPE

Oh, they have robbed me of the hope
  My spirit held so dear;
They will not let me hear that voice
  My soul delights to hear.

They will not let me see that face
  I so delight to see;
And they have taken all thy smiles,
  And all thy love from me.

Well, let them seize on all they can:
  One treasure still is mine,
A heart that loves to think on thee,
  And feels the worth of thine.

DOMESTIC PEACE

Why should such gloomy silence reign,
  And why is all the house so drear,
When neither danger, sickness, pain,
  Nor death, nor want, have entered here?

We are as many as we were
  That other night, when all were gay
And full of hope, and free from care;
  Yet is there something gone away.

The moon without, as pure and calm,
  Is shining as that night she shone;
But now, to us, she brings no balm,
  For something from our hearts is gone.

Something whose absence leaves a void—
  A cheerless want in every heart;
Each feels the bliss of all destroyed,
  And mourns the change—but each apart.

The fire is burning in the grate
  As redly as it used to burn;
But still the hearth is desolate,
  Till mirth, and love, and *peace* return.

'Twas *peace* that flowed from heart to heart,
   With looks and smiles that spoke of heaven,
And gave us language to impart
   The blissful thoughts itself had given.

Domestic peace! best joy of earth,
   When shall we all thy value learn?
White angel, to our sorrowing hearth,
   Return—oh, graciously return!

MIRTH AND MOURNING

'Oh cast away your sorrow;—
   A while, at least, be gay!
If grief must come tomorrow,
   At least, be glad today!

'How can you still be sighing
   When smiles are everywhere?
The little birds are flying
   So blithely through the air;

'The sunshine glows so brightly
   O'er all the blooming earth;
And every heart beats lightly,—
   Each face is full of mirth.'

'I always feel the deepest gloom
   When day most brightly shines:
When Nature shows the fairest bloom,
   My spirit most repines;

'For, in the brightest noontide glow,
   The dungeon's light is dim;
Though freshest winds around us blow,
   No breath can visit him.

'If he must sit in twilight gloom,
   Can I enjoy the sight
Of mountains clad in purple bloom,
   And rocks in sunshine bright?—

'My heart may well be desolate,—
   These tears may well arise
While prison wall and iron grate
   Oppress his weary eyes.'

'But think of him tomorrow,
 And join your comrades now;—
That constant cloud of sorrow
 Ill suits so young a brow.

'Hark, how their merry voices
 Are sounding far and near!
While all the world rejoices
 Can you sit moping here?'

'When others' hearts most lightly bound
 Mine feels the most oppressed;
When smiling faces greet me round
 My sorrow will not rest:

'I think of him whose faintest smile
 Was sunshine to my heart,
Whose lightest word could care beguile
 And blissful thoughts impart;

'I think how he would bless that sun,
 And love this glorious scene;
I think of all that has been done,
 And all that might have been.

'Those sparkling eyes, that blessed me so,
 Are dim with weeping now;
And blighted hope and burning woe
 Have ploughed that marble brow.

'What waste of youth, what hopes destroyed,
 What days of pining care,
What weary nights of comfort void
 Art thou condemned to bear!

'Oh! if my love must suffer so—
 And wholly for my sake—
What marvel that my tears should flow,—
 Or that my heart should break!'

WEEP NOT TOO MUCH

Weep not too much, my darling;
  Sigh not too oft for me;
Say not the face of Nature
  Has lost its charm for thee.
I have enough of anguish
  In my own breast alone;
Thou canst not ease the burden, Love,
  By adding still thine own.

I know the faith and fervour
  Of that true heart of thine;
But I would have it hopeful
  As thou wouldst render mine.
At night, when I lie waking,
  More soothing it will be
To say 'She slumbers calmly now,'
  Than say 'She weeps for me.'

When through the prison grating
  The holy moonbeams shine,
And I am wildly longing
  To see the orb divine
Not crossed, deformed, and sullied
  By those relentless bars
That will not show the crescent moon,
  And scarce the twinkling stars,

It is my only comfort
  To think, that unto thee
The sight is not forbidden
  The face of heaven is free.
If I could think Zerona
  Is gazing upward now
Is gazing with a tearless eye
  A calm unruffled brow;

That moon upon her spirit
  Sheds sweet, celestial balm,
The thought, like Angel's whisper,
  My misery would calm.
And when, at early morning,
  A faint flush comes to me,
Reflected from those glowing skies
  I almost weep to see;

Or when I catch the murmur
  Of gently swaying trees,
Or hear the louder swelling
  Of the soul-inspiring breeze,
And pant to feel its freshness
  Upon my burning brow,
Or sigh to see the twinkling leaf,
  And watch the waving bough;

If, from these fruitless yearnings
  Thou wouldst deliver me,
Say that the charms of Nature
  Are lovely still to thee;
While I am thus repining,
  Oh! let me but believe,
'These pleasures are not lost to her,'
  And I will cease to grieve.

Oh, scorn not Nature's bounties!
  My soul partakes with thee.
Drink bliss from all her fountains,
  Drink for thyself and me!
Say not, 'My soul is buried
  In dungeon gloom with thine;'
But say, *His* heart is here with me;
  His spirit drinks with mine.'

THE POWER OF LOVE

Love, indeed thy strength is mighty
  Thus, alone, such strife to bear—
Three 'gainst one, and never ceasing—
  Death, and Madness, and Despair!

'Tis not my own strength has saved me;
  Health, and hope, and fortitude,
But for love, had long since failed me;
  Heart and soul had sunk subdued.

Often, in my wild impatience,
  I have lost my trust in Heaven,
And my soul has tossed and struggled,
  Like a vessel tempest driven;

But the voice of my belovéd
   In my ear has seemed to say—
'Oh, be patient if thou lov'st me!'
   And the storm has passed away.

When outworn with weary thinking,
   Sight and thought were waxing dim,
And my mind began to wander,
   And my brain began to swim,

Then those hands outstretched to save me
   Seemed to call me back again—
Those dark eyes did so implore me
   To resume my reason's reign,

That I could not but remember
   How her hopes were fixed on me,
And, with one determined effort,
   Rose, and shook my spirit free.

When hope leaves my weary spirit—
   All the power to hold it gone—
That loved voice so loudly prays me,
   'For *my* sake, keep hoping on,'

That, at once my strength renewing,
   Though Despair had crushed me down,
I can burst his bonds asunder,
   And defy his deadliest frown.

When, from nights of restless tossing,
   Days of gloom and pining care,
Pain and weakness, still increasing,
   Seem to whisper 'Death is near,'

And I almost bid him welcome,
   Knowing he would bring release,
Weary of this restless struggle—
   Longing to repose in peace,

Then a glance of fond reproval
   Bids such selfish longings flee
And a voice of matchless music
   Murmurs 'Cherish life for me!'

Roused to newborn strength and courage,
   Pain and grief, I cast away,
Health and life, I keenly follow,
   Mighty Death is held at bay.

Yes, my love, I will be patient!
   Firm and bold my heart shall be:
Fear not—though this life is dreary,
   I can bear it well for thee.

Let our foes still rain upon me
   Cruel wrongs and taunting scorn;
'Tis for thee their hate pursues me,
   And for thee, it shall be borne!

I DREAMT LAST NIGHT

I dreamt last night; and in that dream
   My boyhood's heart was mine again;
These latter years did nothing seem
   With all their mingled joy and pain,

Their thousand deeds of good and ill,
Their hopes which time did not fulfil,
Their glorious moments of success,
Their love that closed in bitterness,

Their hate that grew with growing strength,
Their darling projects—dropped at length,
And higher aims that still prevail,—
For I must perish ere they fail,—

That crowning object of my life,
The end of all my toil and strife,
Source of my virtues and my crimes,
   For which I've toiled and striven in vain,—
But, if I fail a thousand times,
   Still I will toil and strive again:—

Yet even this was then forgot;
My present heart and soul were not:
All the rough lessons life has taught,
   That are become a part of me,
A moment's sleep to nothing brought
   And made me what I used to be.

And I was roaming, light and gay,
Upon a breezy, sunny day,
   A bold and careless youth;
No guilty stain was on my mind;
And, if not over soft or kind,
   My heart was full of truth.

It was a well-known mountain scene;—
Wild steeps, with rugged glens between
I should have thirsted to explore,
Had I not trod them oft before.

A younger boy was with me there.
   His hand upon my shoulder leant;
His heart, like mine, was free from care,
   His breath, with sportive toil, was spent;

For my rough pastimes he would share,
And equal dangers loved to dare,
   Though seldom I would care to vie
In learning's keen pursuit with him;
   I loved free air and open sky
Better than books and tutors grim,

And we had wandered far that day
O'er that forbidden ground away—
Ground, to our rebel feet how dear;
Danger and freedom both were there!—
Had climbed the steep and coursed the dale
Until his strength began to fail.

He bade me pause and breathe a while,
But spoke it with a happy smile.
His lips were parted to inhale
The breeze that swept the ferny dale,

And chased the clouds across the sky,
And waved his locks in passing by,
And fanned my cheek; (so real did seem
This strange, untrue, but truth-like dream;)

And, as we stood, I laughed to see
   His fair young cheek so brightly glow.
He turned his sparkling eyes to me
   With looks no painter's art could show,

Nor words portray;—but earnest mirth,
  And truthful love I there descried;
And, while I thought upon his worth,
  My bosom glowed with joy and pride.

I could have kissed his forehead fair;
  I could nave claspéd him to my heart;
But tenderness with me was rare,
  And I must take a rougher part:

I seized him in my boisterous mirth;
I bore him struggling to the earth
And grappling, strength for strength we strove—
He half in wrath,—I all for love;

But I gave o'er the strife at length,
Ashamed of my superior strength,—
The rather that I marked his eye
Kindle as if a change were nigh.

We paused to breathe a little space,
  Reclining on the heather brae;
But still I gazed upon his face
  To watch the shadow pass away.

I grasped his hand, and it was fled;—
  A smile—a laugh—and all was well:—
Upon my breast he leant his head,
  And into graver talk we fell,—

More serious—yet so blest did seem
  That calm communion then,
That, when I found it but a dream,
  I longed to sleep again.

At first, remembrance slowly woke.
  Surprise, regret, successive rose,
That love's strong cords should thus be broke
  And dearest friends turn deadliest foes.

Then, like a cold, o'erwhelming flood
  Upon my soul it burst—
This heart had thirsted for his blood;
  This hand allayed that thirst!

These eyes had watched, without a tear,
  His dying agony;
These ears, unmoved, had heard his prayer;
This tongue had cursed him suffering there,
  And mocked him bitterly!

Unwonted weakness o'er me crept;
I sighed—nay, weaker still—I *wept!*
Wept, like a woman o'er the deed
  I had been proud to do:—
As I had made his bosom bleed;
  My own was bleeding too.

Back foolish tears!—the man I slew
  Was not the boy I cherished so;
And that young arm that claspéd the friend
  Was not the same that stabbed the foe:
By time and adverse thoughts estranged,
And wrongs and vengeance, both were changed.

Repentance, now, were worse that vain:
  Time's current cannot backward run;
And be the action wrong or right,
  It is for ever done.

Then reap the fruits—I've said his death
  Should be my country's gain:—
If not—then I have spent my breath,
  And spilt his blood in vain:

And I have laboured hard and long,
  But little good obtained;
My foes are many, yet, and strong,
  Not half the battle's gained;

For, still, the greater deeds I've done,
  The more I have to do.
The faster I can journey on,
  The farther I must go.

If Fortune favoured for a while,
I could not rest beneath her smile,
  Nor triumph in success:
When I have gained one river's shore
A wilder torrent, stretched before,
Defies me with its deafening roar;
  And onward I must press.

And, much I doubt, this work of strife,
   In blood and death begun,
Will call for many a victim more
   Before the cause is won.—

Well! my own life, I'd freely give
   Ere I would fail in my design;—
The cause must prosper if I live,
   And I will die if it decline:
Advanced this far, I'll not recede;—
Whether to vanquish or to bleed,
Onward, unchecked, I must proceed.
   Be Death, or Victory mine!

THE LOVER

Gloomily the clouds are sailing
   O'er the dimly moonlit sky;
Dolefully the wind is wailing;
   Not another sound is nigh;

Only I can hear it sweeping
   Heath-clad hill and woodland dale,
And at times the nights' sad weeping
   Sounds above its dying wail.

Now the struggling moonbeams glimmer;
   Now the shadows deeper fall,
Till the dim light, waxing dimmer,
   Scarce reveals yon stately hall.

All beneath its roof are sleeping;
   Such a silence reigns around
I can hear the cold rain steeping
   Dripping roof and plashy ground.

No: not all are wrapped in slumber;
   At yon chamber window stands
One whose years can scarce outnumber
   The tears that dew his claspéd hands.

From the open casement bending
   He surveys the murky skies,
Dreary sighs his bosom rending;
   Hot tears gushing from his eyes.

'Now that Autumn's charms are dying,
   Summer's glories long since gone,
Faded leaves on damp earth lying,
   Hoary winter striding on,—

"Tis no marvel skies are lowering,
   Winds are moaning thus around,
And cold rain, with ceaseless pouring,
   Swells the streams and swamps the ground;

But such wild, such bitter grieving
   Fits not slender boys like thee;
Such deep sighs should not be heaving
   Breasts so young as thine must be.

Life with thee is only springing;
   Summer in thy pathway lies;
Every day is nearer bringing
   June's bright flowers and glowing skies.

Ah, he sees no brighter morrow!
   He is not too young to prove
All the pain and all the sorrow
   That attend the steps of love.

SEVERED AND GONE

Severed and gone, so many years!
   And art thou still so dear to me,
That throbbing heart and burning tears
   Can witness how I cling to thee?

I know that in the narrow tomb
   The form I loved was buried deep,
And left, in silence and in gloom,
   To slumber out its dreamless sleep.

I know the corner where it lies,
   Is but a dreary place of rest:
The charnel moisture never dries
   From the dark flagstones o'er its breast,

For there the sunbeams never shine,
   Nor ever breathes the freshening air,
But not for this do I repine;
   For my belovéd is not there.

Oh, no! I do not think of thee
  As festering there in slow decay:
'Tis this sole thought oppresses me,
  That thou art gone so far away.

For ever gone; for I, by night,
  Have prayed, within my silent room,
That Heaven would grant a burst of light
  Its cheerless darkness to illume;

And give thee to my longing eyes,
  A moment, as thou shinest now,
Fresh from thy mansion in the skies,
  With all its glories on thy brow.

Wild was the wish, intense the gaze
  I fixed upon the murky air,
Expecting, half, a kindling blaze
  Would strike my raptured vision there,

A shape these human nerves would thrill,
  A majesty that might appal,
Did not thy earthly likeness, still,
  Gleam softly, gladly, through it all.

False hope! vain prayer! it might not be
  That thou shouldst visit earth again.
I called on Heaven—I called on thee,
  And watched, and waited—all in vain.

Had I one shining tress of thine,
  How it would bless these longing eyes!
Or if thy pictured form were mine,
  What gold should rob me of the prize?

A few cold words on yonder stone,
  A corpse as cold as they can be—
Vain words, and mouldering dust, alone—
  Can this be all that's left of thee?

Oh, no! thy spirit lingers still
  Where'er thy sunny smile was seen:
There's less of darkness, less of chill
  On earth, than if thou hadst not been.

Thou breathest in my bosom yet,
   And dwellest in my beating heart;
And, while I cannot quite forget,
   Thou, darling, canst not quite depart.

Though, freed from sin, and grief, and pain
   Thou drinkest now the bliss of Heaven,
Thou didst not visit earth in vain;
   And from us, yet, thou art not riven.

Life seems more sweet that thou didst live,
   And men more true that thou wert one:
Nothing is lost that thou didst give,
   Nothing destroyed that thou hast done.

Earth hath received thine earthly part;
   Thine heavenly flame has heavenward flown;
But both still linger in my heart,
   Still live, and not in mine alone.

THE THREE GUIDES

Spirit of Earth! thy hand is chill:
   I've felt its icy clasp;
And, shuddering, I remember still
   That stony-hearted grasp.
Thine eye bids love and joy depart:
   Oh, turn its gaze from me!
It presses down my shrinking heart;
   I will not walk with thee!

"Wisdom is mine," I've heard thee say:
   "Beneath my searching eye
All mist and darkness melt away,
   Phantoms and fables fly.
Before me truth can stand alone,
   The naked, solid truth;
And man matured by worth will own,
   If I am shunned by youth.

"Firm is my tread, and sure though slow;
  My footsteps never slide;
And he that follows me shall know
  I am the surest guide."
Thy boast is vain; but were it true
  That thou couldst safely steer
Life's rough and devious pathway through,
  Such guidance I should fear.

How could I bear to walk for aye,
  With eyes to earthward prone,
O'er trampled weeds and miry clay,
  And sand and flinty stone;
Never the glorious view to greet
  Of hill and dale, and sky;
To see that Nature's charms are sweet,
  Or feel that Heaven is nigh?

If in my heart arose a spring,
  A gush of thought divine,
At once stagnation thou wouldst bring
  With that cold touch of thine.
If, glancing up, I sought to snatch
  But one glimpse of the sky,
My baffled gaze would only catch
  Thy heartless, cold grey eye.

If to the breezes wandering near,
  I listened eagerly,
And deemed an angel's tongue to hear
  That whispered hope to me,
That heavenly music would be drowned
  In thy harsh, droning voice;
Nor inward thought, nor sight, nor sound,
  Might my sad soul rejoice.

Dull is thine ear, unheard by thee
  The still, small voice of Heaven;
Thine eyes are dim and cannot see
  The helps that God has given.
There is a bridge o'er every flood
  Which thou canst not perceive;
A path through every tangled wood,
  But thou wilt not believe.

Striving to make thy way by force,
   Toil-spent and bramble-torn,
Thou'lt fell the tree that checks thy course,
   And burst through brier and thorn:
And, pausing by the river's side,
   Poor reasoner! thou wilt deem,
By casting pebbles in its tide,
   To cross the swelling stream.

Right through the flinty rock thou'lt try
   Thy toilsome way to bore,
Regardless of the pathway nigh
   That would conduct thee o'er
Not only art thou, then, unkind,
   And freezing cold to me,
But unbelieving, deaf, and blind:
   I will not walk with thee!

Spirit of Pride! thy wings are strong,
   Thine eyes like lightning shine;
Ecstatic joys to thee belong,
   And powers almost divine.
But 'tis a false, destructive blaze
   Within those eyes I see;
Turn hence their fascinating gaze;
   I will not follow thee.

"Coward and fool!" thou mayst reply,
   Walk on the common sod;
Go, trace with timid foot and eye
   The steps by others trod.
'Tis best the beaten path to keep,
   The ancient faith to hold;
To pasture with thy fellow-sheep,
   And lie within the fold.

"Cling to the earth, poor grovelling worm;
   'Tis not for thee to soar
Against the fury of the storm,
   Amid the thunder's roar!
There's glory in that daring strife
   Unknown, undreamt by thee;
There's speechless rapture in the life
   Of those who follow me.

Yes, I have seen thy votaries oft,
   Upheld by thee their guide,
In strength and courage mount aloft
   The steepy mountain-side;
I've seen them stand against the sky,
   And gazing from below,
Beheld thy lightning in their eye
   Thy triumph on their brow.

Oh, I have felt what glory then,
   What transport must be theirs!
So far above their fellow-men,
   Above their toils and cares;
Inhaling Nature's purest breath,
   Her riches round them spread,
The wide expanse of earth beneath,
   Heaven's glories overhead!

But I have seen them helpless, dash'd
   Down to a bloody grave,
And still thy ruthless eye has flash'd,
   Thy strong hand did not save;
I've seen some o'er the mountain's brow
   Sustain'd awhile by thee,
O'er rocks of ice and hills of snow
   Bound fearless, wild, and free.

Bold and exultant was their mien,
   While thou didst cheer them on;
But evening fell,—and then, I ween,
   Their faithless guide was gone.
Alas! how fared thy favourites then,—
   Lone, helpless, weary, cold?
Did ever wanderer find again
   The path he left of old?

Where is their glory, where the pride
   That swelled their hearts before?
Where now the courage that defied
   The mightiest tempest's roar?
What shall they do when night grows black,
   When angry storms arise?
Who now will lead them to the track
   Thou taught'st them to despise?

Spirit of Pride, it needs not this
   To make me shun thy wiles,
Renounce thy triumph and thy bliss,
   Thy honours and thy smiles!
Bright as thou art, and bold, and strong,
   That fierce glance wins not me,
And I abhor thy scoffing tongue—
   I will not follow thee!

Spirit of Faith! be thou my guide,
   O clasp my hand in thine,
And let me never quit thy side;
   Thy comforts are divine!
Earth calls thee blind, misguided one,—
   But who can shew like thee
Forgotten things that have been done,
   And things that are to be?

Secrets conceal'd from Nature's ken,
   Who like thee can declare?
Or who like thee to erring men
   God's holy will can bear?
Pride scorns thee for thy lowly mien,—
   But who like thee can rise
Above this toilsome, sordid scene,
   Beyond the holy skies?

Meek is thine eye and soft thy voice,
   But wondrous is thy might,
To make the wretched soul rejoice,
   To give the simple light!
And still to all that seek thy way
   This magic power is given,—
E'en while their footsteps press the clay,
   Their souls ascend to heaven.

Danger surrounds them,—pain and woe
   Their portion here must be,
But only they that trust thee know
   What comfort dwells with thee;
Strength to sustain their drooping pow'rs,
   And vigour to defend,—
Thou pole-star of my darkest hours
   Affliction's firmest friend!

Day does not always mark our way,
　　Night's shadows oft appal,
But lead me, and I cannot stray,—
　　Hold me, I shall not fall;
Sustain me, I shall never faint,
　　How rough soe'er may be
My upward road,—nor moan, nor plaint
　　Shall mar my trust in thee.

Narrow the path by which we go,
　　And oft it turns aside
From pleasant meads where roses blow,
　　And peaceful waters glide;
Where flowery turf lies green and soft,
　　And gentle gales are sweet,
To where dark mountains frown aloft,
　　Hard rocks distress the feet,—

Deserts beyond lie bleak and bare,
　　And keen winds round us blow;
But if thy hand conducts me there,
　　The way is right, I know.
I have no wish to turn away;
　　My spirit does not quail,—
How can it while I hear thee say,
　　"Press forward and prevail!"

Even above the tempest's swell
　　I hear thy voice of love,—
Of hope and peace, I hear thee tell,
　　And that blest home above;
Through pain and death I can rejoice.
　　If but thy strength be mine,—
Earth hath no music like thy voice,
　　Life owns no joy like thine!

Spirit of Faith, I'll go with thee!
　　Thou, if I hold thee fast,
Wilt guide, defend, and strengthen me,
　　And bear me home at last;
By thy help all things I can do,
　　In thy strength all things bear,—
Teach me, for thou art just and true,
　　Smile on me, thou art fair!

FAREWELL TO THEE! BUT NOT FAREWELL

Farewell to thee! but not farewell
   To all my fondest thoughts of thee:
Within my heart they still shall dwell;
   And they shall cheer and comfort me.

Oh, beautiful, and full of grace!
   If thou hadst never met mine eye,
I had not dreamed a living face
   Could fancied charms so far outvie.

If I may ne'er behold again
   That form and face so dear to me,
Nor hear thy voice, still would I fain
   Preserve, for aye, their memory.

That voice, the magic of whose tone
   Can wake an echo in my breast,
Creating feelings that, alone,
   Can make my tranced spirit blest.

That laughing eye, whose sunny beam
   My memory would not cherish less;—
And oh, that smile! whose joyous gleam
   Nor mortal language can express.

Adieu, but let me cherish, still,
   The hope with which I cannot part.
Contempt may wound, and coldness chill,
   But still it lingers in my heart.

And who can tell but Heaven, at last,
   May answer all my thousand prayers,
And bid the future pay the past
   With joy for anguish, smiles for tears?

SELF-COMMUNION

'The mist is resting on the hill;
   The smoke is hanging in the air;
The very clouds are standing still:
   A breathless calm broods everywhere.
Thou pilgrim through this vale of tears,
   Thou, too, a little moment cease
Thy anxious toil and fluttering fears,
   And rest thee, for a while, in peace.'

'I would, but Time keeps working still
And moving on for good or ill:
   He will not rest or stay.
In pain or ease, in smiles or tears,
He still keeps adding to my years
   And stealing life away.
His footsteps in the ceaseless sound
   Of yonder clock I seem to hear,
That through this stillness so profound
   Distinctly strikes the vacant ear.
For ever striding on and on,
   He pauses not by night or day;
And all my life will soon be gone
   As these past years have slipped away.
He took my childhood long ago,
And then my early youth; and lo,
   He steals away my prime!
I cannot see how fast it goes,
But well my inward spirit knows
   The wasting power of time.'

'Time steals thy moments, drinks thy breath,
   Changes and wastes thy mortal frame;
But though he gives the clay to death,
   He cannot touch the inward flame.
Nay, though he steals thy years away,
   Their memory is left thee still,
And every month and every day
   Leaves some effect of good or ill.
The wise will find in Memory's store
A help for that which lies before
   To guide their course aright;
Then, hush thy plaints and calm thy fears;
Look back on these departed years,
   And, say, what meets thy sight?'

'I see, far back, a helpless child,
   Feeble and full of causeless fears,
Simple and easily beguiled
   To credit all it hears.
More timid than the wild wood-dove,
   Yet trusting to another's care,
And finding in protecting love
   Its only refuge from despair,—
Its only balm for every woe,
The only bliss its soul can know;—
   Still hiding in its breast.

A tender heart too prone to weep,
A love so earnest, strong, and deep
   It could not be expressed.
Poor helpless thing! what can it do
   Life's stormy cares and toils among;—
How tread this weary desert through
   That awes the brave and tires the strong?
Where shall it centre so much trust
   Where truth maintains so little sway,
Where seeming fruit is bitter dust,
   And kisses oft to death betray?

How oft must sin and falsehood grieve
A heart so ready to believe,
   And willing to admire!
With strength so feeble, fears so strong,
Amid this selfish bustling throng,
   How will it faint and tire!
That tender love so warm and deep,
   How can it flourish here below?
What bitter floods of tears must steep
   The stony soil where it would grow!
Oh, earth! a rocky breast is thine—
   A hard soil and a cruel clime,
Where tender plants must droop and pine,
   Or alter with transforming time.
That soul, that clings to sympathy,
As ivy clasps the forest tree,
   How can it stand alone?
That heart so prone to overflow
E'en at the thought of others' woe,
   How will it bear its own?
How, if a sparrow's death can wring
   Such bitter tear-floods from the eye,
Will it behold the suffering
   Of struggling, lost humanity?
The torturing pain, the pining grief,
   The sin-degraded misery,
The anguish that defies relief?'

'Look back again—What dost thou see?'

'I see one kneeling on the sod,
   With infant hands upraised to Heaven,
A young heart feeling after God,
   Oft baffled, never backward driven.
Mistaken oft, and oft astray,
It strives to find the narrow way,

But gropes and toils alone:
That inner life of strife and tears,
Of kindling hopes and lowering fears
    To none but God is known.
'Tis better thus; for man would scorn
    Those childish prayers, those artless cries,
That darkling spirit tossed and torn,
    But God will not despise!
We may regret such waste of tears
    Such darkly toiling misery,
Such 'wildering doubts and harrowing fears,
    Where joy and thankfulness should be;
But wait, and Heaven will send relief.
    Let patience have her perfect work:
Lo, strength and wisdom spring from grief,
    And joys behind afflictions lurk!
It asked for light, and it is heard;
    God grants that struggling soul repose
And, guided by His holy word,
    It wiser than its teachers grows.
It gains the upward path at length,
And passes on from strength to strength,
    Leaning on Heaven the while:
Night's shades departing one by one,
It sees at last the rising sun,
    And feels his cheering smile.
In all its darkness and distress
    For light it sought, to God it cried;
And through the pathless wilderness,
    He was its comfort and its guide.'

'So was it, and so will it be:
Thy God will guide and strengthen thee;
    His goodness cannot fail.
The sun that on thy morning rose
Will light thee to the evening's close,
    Whatever storms assail.'

'*God* alters not; but Time on me
    A wide and wondrous change has wrought:
And in these parted years I see
    Cause for grave care and saddening thought.
I see that time, and toil, and truth,
    An inward hardness can impart,—
Can freeze the generous blood of youth,
    And steel full fast the tender heart.'

'Bless God for that divine decree!—
That hardness comes with misery,
   And suffering deadens pain;
That at the frequent sight of woe
E'en Pity's tears forget to flow,
   If reason still remain!
Reason, with conscience by her side,
   But gathers strength from toil and truth;
And she will prove a surer guide
   Than those sweet instincts of our youth.
Thou that hast known such anguish sore
   In weeping where thou couldst not bless,
Canst *thou* that softness so deplore—
   That suffering, shrinking tenderness?
Thou that hast felt what cankering care
A loving heart is doomed to bear,
   Say, how canst thou regret
That fires unfed must fall away,
Long droughts can dry the softest clay,
   And cold will cold beget?'

'Nay, but 'tis hard to feel that chill
   Come creeping o'er the shuddering heart.
Love may be full of pain, but still,
   'Tis sad to see it so depart,—
To watch that fire whose genial glow
   Was formed to comfort and to cheer,
For want of fuel, fading so,
   Sinking to embers dull and drear,—
To see the soft soil turned to stone
   For lack of kindly showers,—
To see those yearnings of the breast,
Pining to bless and to be blessed,
Drop withered, frozen one by one,
Till, centred in itself alone,
   It wastes its blighted powers.

Oh, I have known a wondrous joy
   In early friendship's pure delight,—
A genial bliss that could not cloy—
   My sun by day, my moon by night.
Absence, indeed, was sore distress,
   And thought of death was anguish keen,
And there was cruel bitterness
   When jarring discords rose between;
And sometimes it was grief to know
   My fondness was but half returned.

But this was nothing to the woe
 With which another truth was learned:—
That I must check, or nurse apart,
Full many an impulse of the heart
 And many a darling thought:
What my soul worshipped, sought, and prized,
Were slighted, questioned, or despised;—
 This pained me more than aught.
And as my love the warmer glowed
 The deeper would that anguish sink,
That this dark stream between us flowed,
 Though both stood bending o'er its brink;
Until, as last, I learned to bear
 A colder heart within my breast;
To share such thoughts as I could share,
 And calmly keep the rest.
I saw that they were sundered now,
 The trees that at the root were one:
They yet might mingle leaf and bough,
 But still the stems must stand alone.
Oh, love is sweet of every kind!
 'Tis sweet the helpless to befriend,
To watch the young unfolding mind,
 To guide, to shelter, and defend:
To lavish tender toil and care,
 And ask for nothing back again,
But that our smiles a blessing bear
 And all our toil be not in vain.
And sweeter far than words can tell
Their love whose ardent bosoms swell
 With thoughts they need not hide;
Where fortune frowns not on their joy,
And Prudence seeks not to destroy,
 Nor Reason to deride.

Whose love may freely gush and flow,
 Unchecked, unchilled by doubt or fear,
For in their inmost hearts they know
 It is not vainly nourished there.
They know that in a kindred breast
 Their long desires have found a home,
Where heart and soul may kindly rest,
 Weary and lorn no more to roam.
  Their dreams of bliss were not in vain,
  As they love they are loved again,
And they can bless as they are blessed.

Oh, vainly might I seek to show
The joys from happy love that flow!
The warmest words are all too cold
The secret transports to unfold
Of simplest word or softest sigh,
Or from the glancing of an eye
    To say what rapture beams;
One look that bids our fears depart,
And well assures the trusting heart.
It beats not in the world alone—
Such speechless rapture I have known,
    But only in my dreams.

My life has been a morning sky
    Where Hope her rainbow glories cast
O'er kindling vapours far and nigh:
    And, if the colours faded fast,
Ere one bright hue had died away
    Another o'er its ashes gleamed;
And if the lower clouds were grey,
    The mists above more brightly beamed.
But not for long;—at length behold,
    Those tints less warm, less radiant grew;
Till but one streak of paly gold
    Glimmered through clouds of saddening hue.
And I am calmly waiting, now,
    To see that also pass away,
And leave, above the dark hill's brow,
    A rayless arch of sombre grey.'

'So must it fare with all thy race
    Who seek in earthly things their joy:
So fading hopes lost hopes shall chase
    Till Disappointment all destroy.
But they that fix their hopes on high
Shall, in the blue-refulgent sky,
    The sun's transcendent light,
Behold a purer, deeper glow
Than these uncertain gleams can show,
    However fair or bright.
Oh, weak of heart! why thus deplore
    That Truth will Fancy's dreams destroy?
Did I not tell thee, years before,
    Life was for labour, not for joy?
Cease, selfish spirit, to repine;
    O'er thine own ills no longer grieve;
Lo, there are sufferings worse than thine,

Which thou mayst labour to relieve.
If Time indeed too swiftly flies,
Gird on thine armour, haste, arise,
   For thou hast much to do;—
To lighten woe, to trample sin,
And foes without and foes within
   To combat and subdue.
Earth hath too much of sin and pain:
The bitter cup—the binding chain
   Dost thou indeed lament?
Let not thy weary spirit sink;
But strive—not by one drop or link
   The evil to augment.
Strive rather thou, by peace and joy,
The bitter poison to destroy,
   The cruel chain to break.

Oh, strive! and if thy strength be small,
Strive yet the more, and spend it all
   For Love and Wisdom's sake!'
'Oh, I have striven both hard and long
But many are my foes and strong.
My gains are light—my progress slow;
For hard's the way I have to go,
And my worst enemies, I know,
   Are these within my breast;
And it is hard to toil for aye,—
Through sultry noon and twilight grey
   To toil and never rest.'

'There is a rest beyond the grave,
   A lasting rest from pain and sin,
Where dwell the faithful and the brave;
   But they must strive who seek to win.'

"Show me that rest—I ask no more.
Oh, drive these misty doubts away;
And let me see that sunny shore,
   However far away!
However wide this rolling sea,
However wild my passage be,
Howe'er my bark be tempest tossed,
   May it but reach that haven fair,
   May I but land and wander there,
With those that I have loved and lost:
With such a glorious hope in view,
I'll gladly toil and suffer too.
Rest *without* toil I would not ask;

I would not shun the hardest task:
Toil is my glory—Grief my gain,
If God's approval they obtain.
Could I but hear my Saviour say,—
    "I know thy patience and thy love;
How thou hast held the narrow way,
For my sake laboured night and day,
    And watched, and striven with them that strove;
And still hast borne, and didst not faint,"—
    Oh, this would be reward indeed!'

'Press forward, then, without complaint;
    Labour and love—and such shall be thy meed.'

THE NARROW WAY

Believe not those who say
    The upward path is smooth,
Lest thou shouldst stumble in the way,
    And faint before the truth.

It is the only road
    Unto the realms of joy;
But he who seeks that blest abode
    Must all his powers employ.

Bright hopes and pure delight
    Upon his course may beam,
And there, amid the sternest heights,
    The sweetest flowerets gleam.

On all her breezes borne,
    Earth yields no scents like those;
But he that dares not gasp the thorn
    Should never crave the rose.

Arm—arm thee for the fight!
    Cast useless loads away;
Watch through the darkest hours of night;
    Toil through the hottest day.

Crush pride into the dust,
    Or thou must needs be slack;
And trample down rebellious lust,
    Or it will hold thee back.

Seek not thy honour here;
   Waive pleasure and renown;
The world's dread scoff undaunted bear,
   And face its deadliest frown.

To labour and to love,
   To pardon and endure,
To lift thy heart to God above,
   And keep thy conscience pure;

Be this thy constant aim,
   Thy hope, thy chief delight;
What matter who should whisper blame
   Or who should scorn or slight?

What matter, if thy God approve,
   And if, within thy breast,
Thou feel the comfort of His love,
   The earnest of His rest?

FRAGMENT

Yes I will take a cheerful tone
   And feign to share their heartless glee,
But I would rather weep alone
   Than laugh amid their revelry.

LAST LINES

I hoped, that with the brave and strong,
   My portioned task might lie;
To toil amid the busy throng,
   With purpose pure and high.

But God has fixed another part,
   And He has fixed it well;
I said so with my bleeding heart,
   When first the anguish fell.

Thou, God, hast taken our delight,
   Our treasured hope away:
Thou bid'st us now weep through the night
   And sorrow through the day.

These weary hours will not be lost,
   These days of misery,
These nights of darkness, anguish-tost,
   Can I but turn to Thee.

With secret labour to sustain
   In humble patience every blow;
To gather fortitude from pain,
   And hope and holiness from woe.

Thus let me serve Thee from my heart,
   Whate'er may be my written fate:
Whether thus early to depart,
   Or yet a while to wait.

If Thou shouldst bring me back to life,
   More humbled I should be;
More wise—more strengthened for the strife—
   More apt to lean on Thee.

Should death be standing at the gate,
   Thus should I keep my vow:
But, Lord! whatever be my fate,
   Oh, let me serve Thee now!

THE END

Lightning Source UK Ltd.
Milton Keynes UK
UKOW03f0632160517
301301UK00002B/415/P